Crime and Punishment in the North East

by Lorna Windham

Introduction

An interest in the history of crime in the north east led to the writing of this book. As I researched I got to know more about individuals, their crimes and their punishments. History came alive when they became my focus.

Today we rely on forensic evidence such as DNA, blood groups and fingerprints to help us solve crimes. In the past there was no scientific investigation, trials depended on witness statements, memory and or superstition. This was the case with the witch trials which took place in Newcastle where innocents were hanged.

Those accused of crimes such as petty larceny may have been criminalised by a system of justice that relied on circumstantial evidence, the accuser being honest, and or having a good memory. Mistakes will have been made and punishments unforgiving and brutal.

Tracing the lives of some of these northerners, particularly those who were transported to the far outposts of the British Empire has been a fascinating process.

I remember chatting to local author, Yvonne Young, and saying I'd like to find out more about the history of the area. Her reply was, 'Why don't you then?' So I did.

Lorna Windham

Acknowledgements

I'd like to extend my sincere thanks to the staff at Newcastle Central Library for their efficient service; the staff at Tyne and Wear Archives for three photographs from the Newcastle Gaol, Collection of Prison Forms and Photographs 1873; fellow author and poet Yvonne Young for her photographs and research; super sleuth John Gallon for all his hard work; Jill Forster for her research in Australia; fellow author Barry Redfern for his advice and photographs; my publisher Andrew Clark for believing in me and the project, and my husband and family for their support.

The publisher would like to thank the following for supplying illustrations:

Alan Brett, Paul Heslop, George Nairn, Harry Wynne and John Yearnshire.

A Victorian Police Sergeant.

Copyright Lorna Windham 2010

First published in 2010 by

Summerhill Books
PO Box 1210 Newcastle-upon-Tyne NE99 4AH

Email: summerhillbooks@yahoo.co.uk

www.summerhillbooks.co.uk

ISBN: 978-1-906721-34-3

Printed by: CVN Print Ltd, Maxwell Street, South Shields

Crimes

Today, many people believe we live in a time of rising crime; that it's no longer safe to walk the streets of our inner cities. They compare what happens now unfavourably with an imagined past.

In fact in the 13th-16th centuries the borders: Berwickshire, Cumberland, Dumfriesshire, Northumberland, Roxburghshire, Selkirk and Westmorland were no go areas for all but warring reivers (raiders) who acted outside the law and raided at will. In the 17th century moss troopers (brigands) appeared to follow suit. Those who were appointed by the Crown to uphold the law, Country Keepers and their assistants seemed incapable of doing so to any great extent or were corrupt and easily bribed.

The 18th-20th centuries had a volatile mix of upper, middle and lower classes divided by low pay, poor education, grinding poverty, overcrowded slums, poor health and sanitation on a scale that we in the 21st century can hardly comprehend. It was a breeding ground for unrest and crime.

Many crimes were reported in local papers such as the weekly *Newcastle Courant* published from 1791-1926. It merged with *The Newcastle Journal* in 1876. Its circulation was Durham, Newcastle, the Northern Counties, North and South Shields and Sunderland. Eneas Mackenzie in his book, *A descriptive and historical account of the town and county of Newcastle upon Tyne including Gateshead* (1827) also noted many crimes.

'Gin Lane' – an engraving by William Hogarth showing the seedy side of life in 18th century England.

Newcastle Courant

Crimes were reported under the heading, 'HUE AND CRY'.

NEWCASTLE UPON TYNE A STABLE BROKEN INTO
Whereas on Thursday night, a Stable in the Manor Chair in this ... Saddle with plain stirrups, tin'd over leather buttons; a pair of ... coat, with metal buttons were stolen there'out, – Whoever will ... persons that committed the above offence, shall receive TWO GUINEAS ... APPLYING TO THE Printer of this paper.

Newcastle, 21st January, 1786.
A CAUTION
On Wednesday afternoon between five and six o'clock, a woman called at a house in this town, and pretended she was sent by a Gentleman to borrow a great coat, which she obtained, and has not since been heard of. – It is hoped, this be a caution to servants to prevent like frauds.

In modern times we rely on the state and 'Crime Stoppers' to offer rewards for the capture of criminals. In the 18th century many private individuals who were victims of crime, clubbed together to pay for advertisements which could bring the criminals to justice.

'Newcastle Courant'

HARRATON TOWNSHIP ASSOCIATION
For bringing to justice ROGUES and THIEVES.
At a meeting, held this date at Mr. John Daker's at Fatfield, it is unanimously resolved, that we, whose names are hereunto subscribed, shall and do enter into a subscription for the purpose of prosecuting to conviction, persons guilty of Theft, Burglary, and other kinds of Felony, upon any Persons, Property or Effects, in the town-ship or constablery of Harraton, in the county of Durham. Also do agree to pay any person or persons, who shall give information on Oath, before any of his Majesty's Justices of the Peace for the said county of Durham, against any offenders, a handsome gratuity, on conviction of such offender or offenders. The above is also meant to extend to the detection and prosecution of any person or persons, who may hereafter receive any goods, knowing the same to be stolen from any of us; as also to all Garden Breakers, &c. As witness our hands, the day and year above written.

19th century Tyneside – A bustling River Tyne shows that this is the age of sail and steam.

15th September, 1746 – Soldier Shot!

Some people received the ultimate penalty, whilst others had a lucky escape.

First light or sunrise was the traditional time for a firing squad, hence the phrase, 'shot at dawn'. The squad would be composed of several soldiers ordered to fire simultaneously at a hooded or blindfolded victim who could request that their eyes be uncovered. They would be tied either sitting or standing to a stake.

Alexander Anthony, 23 was a Lincolnshire man and soldier in Brigadier Cholomondeley's regiment. Wounded and captured at the Battle of Fontenoy, he later enlisted in Fitz-James' horse and fought bravely at the Battle of Culloden. Quartered in

Newcastle, he was shot as a traitor, on the Town Moor, because he entered the French service. (Mackenzie 1827)

The process was quick and no one knew who fired the lethal bullet. Occasionally one or more members of a squad would be issued a 'conscience round' a blank cartridge inserted in the weapon, again to allay feelings of responsibility for the death of a fellow soldier. The difference between live and blank rounds would be known by expert marksmen, as the blank round has lower recoil, but psychologically it perhaps allowed them to have a get out clause. The 'coup de grace', a single shot to the head would be given if the soldier was still alive.

Soldiers in the 21st century are volunteers and in early times, men peacefully enlisted into the forces by accepting the 'king's shilling'. However, in the 16th-18th centuries the Crown used press gangs to forcibly 'press' or 'impress' men into the navy or army. The Impress Service operated from a headquarters named Rendezvous in every port in Great Britain. The senior officer was called the Regulating officer, in a large port this would be a captain and in a small port a lieutenant. On land, local thugs, rarely sailors were hired as 'gangers' and formed a press gang who would roam the countryside looking for unfortunate souls to 'press'.

Travel expenses were paid. Senior officers were given 3d per mile; 1d went to each man in the gang and up to 10 shillings was paid for each man pressed. A wealthy man would often bribe the press gang to let him go. The poor had no way out. Desertion was most likely at the start of a man's service. It's not surprising that desertion from the army and the navy was common.

20th February, 1758 – Press Gang!

A soldier, William Bland, in General Buckland's second battalion, had been quartered in Newcastle and was shot for desertion on the Town Moor. He hadn't volunteered to join the army he'd been 'impressed'.

1813 Press Gangs

In the 19th century a press gang in The Close, Newcastle, grabbed a youth called Bell. On spying his sister, whilst he was waiting with other pressed men to be put on a ship, he asked if he could talk to her. They exchanged clothes allowing him to escape dressed as a woman. She was taken to a magistrate, but later released.

Wealthy people lived in grand houses in The Close, till noise, pollution and overcrowding, persuaded them to move away. It was one of Newcastle's most ancient streets and was just behind the quayside. The account below of the goings on in the 18th century gives us a rare glimpse of what it might have been like.

21st September, 1758 – Killer Sheep!

'a sheep, being pursued by a butcher's dog, ran down a lane in The Close, and, in jumping into the river, threw two dyers, named Clowney and Porteus, who were washing cloth, into the Tyne. They were both drowned.'
(Mackenzie 1827)

The Water Tower, The Close, Newcastle, 1846.

1753 – Child Murder!

Many children today are born outside marriage with no stigma attached to them or their parents. This was not the case in earlier times.

Traditionally illegitimate births were thought of as shameful. If an infant died, the mother could be accused of murder, even though the baby may have been still born or died from natural causes.

The 1743-4 Act of Parliament punished unmarried mothers by whipping. It has been suggested that the increase in illegitimate births in the 18th century was because of the rapid rise in ale houses between the 1730s and 1780s. Recently, many women have blamed their unwanted pregnancies on their being drunk at the time of conception.

In 1753, Lord Hardwicke's Marriage Act required people to be married with banns or a license; to have parental agreement for minors; witnesses; an authorized clergyman and a record in a Marriage Register. This reinforced the sanctity of marriage and legitimate births, but on the other hand ensured the

A whipping post.

shaming of an unmarried woman and her illegitimate child in front of the community in which she lived. It was recorded that a woman, 'Dorothy Catenby was condemned at the Newcastle assizes and executed for the murder of her bastard child.' We'll never know whether Dorothy's child was still born, died soon after birth or was murdered. (Mackenzie 1827)

1753 – Rape!

Today we try to protect the victims of rape, they remain anonymous, but their actions are still challenged. In the 18th century rape was a felony. It was also unique, because the trial concentrated on the victim's actions and state of mind as well as that of the defendant.

17th century Lord Chief Justice Sir Matthew Hale is often quoted when commenting on the subject, 'rape … is an accusation easily to be made and hard to be proved, and harder to be defended by the party accused, tho never so innocent.' He also said, 'In a rape case it is the victim, not the defendant, who is on trial.'

In 1753 Elizabeth Hall was raped at Elsdon and died. Tried and condemned to death, three men were eventually pardoned. (Mackenzie 1827)

1756 – Pardoned

Though we no longer have capital punishment in Britain, we did once. On one occasion a murderer, Richard Curtis, was sentenced to be hanged at the assizes for the murder of William Atkinson. His supposed accomplice Charles Cowling escaped the noose. A town's serjeant tried to arrest Cowling 'by an escape warrant; but he was reprieved because the warrant was void'. He was afterwards pardoned. (Mackenzie 1827)

THE PIOUS PUBLIC-HOUSE.

(WHERE YOU MAY GET ADULTERATED BEER AND GIN.)

A Place in which the Great Brewers DON'T see any Particular Harm !

Left: Alcohol has often been blamed for society's ills. Here is the magazine Punch's view of public houses.

1786 – Pitmen Absconded

To work in the pit you had to sign a contract called a bond. This was probably read out to a mass meeting of pitmen. However, it may not have been read or explained to some them. Most pitmen, being illiterate, in the 18th century would have signed the bond with an X. It was rare to receive a copy of the bond. A cash prize was offered to the first man to sign and everyone who followed suit was given 'binding money' and beer.

The bond stated they had to work for the master of the pit usually for a period of 11 months and 15 days. It didn't guarantee employment or that this would be full or continuous. Absenteeism, poor work, poor punctuality and so on were rewarded with a fine. There wasn't necessarily an agreed wage, though sometimes a pit house was provided.

Absconding was a breach of the bond by the employee and was a criminal offence under the Master and Servant Act. This usually meant a prison sentence. Unfairly, it was only a civil offence if the master breached the bond.

As seen in the *Newcastle Courant* below, in 1786 the owners of Walbottle Pit, Callerton Pit, Wylam Colliery and Throckley Colliery offered a reward for pitmen who'd absconded from their pits.

19th century pitmen from Hebburn on strike. An illustration from the Daily Sketch.

PITMEN ABSCONDED

Whereas William Dowson, John Wilson, John Atkinson, John Anderson, are legally hired to work at Walbottle Colliery to the 26th day of October 1786. John Robson, Mark Morris, John Hall, William Minto, Edward Marshall, Peter Watson, Robert Dixon, Matthew Wilson-Daniel Blyth, John Blyth, supposed gone to Scotland, are also hired to work at Callerton Colliery to the 11th November, 1786. Walter Elliot, Robert Elliot, John Elliot, Robert Neaven, Thomas Neaven, George Rule, Robert Roddison, (alias White Sark), John Roddison, and Joseph Leamen, are likewise hired Pitmen to work at Wylam Colliery to the 22d November, 1786, and Richard Middleton hired to work at the said Colliery to the 22d inst. George Grey, and Thomas Smith, hired to work at Throckley Colliery, to the 24th October, 1786, all in the county of Northumberland.

NOTICE is hereby Given, that the Owners of the above Collieries have entered into an association to prosecute any person or persons employing all or any of the said hired workmen to the utmost rigour of the law; and in order to apprehend the said Pitmen, a reward of ONE GUINEA is hereby offered, over and above reasonable expenses, for each Pitman, upon conviction, to be paid by Charles Nixon, of Walbottle, or John Bedlington, of Throckley aforesaid.

The miners would have been mainly uneducated and driven by poverty and hunger. Bribed by the thought of 'free' alcohol they would probably have had very little idea of the horrific conditions underground where they faced possible injury, permanent disability or death. Unable to obtain other employment, some would have had little choice, but to sign the Bond, others might have found illegal activities such as pickpocketing a more attractive alternative to the back breaking work in the pit.

27th June, 1788 – Pickpocket Caught!

Pickpockets in the 18th century were called 'divers'. They had to be quick, with nimble, dextrous fingers. Apprentice pickpockets were given 10 guineas so that they could live until they raised money themselves from their illegal employment. They

were taken to likely places or events to observe the ploys of the more experienced in this craft when they stole purses and jewellery. Having found a victim, the pickpocket might fake an illness or pretend they needed help. Ironically, the helper, whilst coming to their aid, would have articles of value removed from their person. Sometimes valuable articles were stolen, occasionally the victim was beaten to the ground.

This is an old postcard titled 'A Quaint Corner in Newcastle', however, it shows the poverty of the city with the children without any shoes. Poverty such as this was a breeding ground for crime.

An infamous pickpocket, Barrington was caught and charged with attempting to steal a watch from a Mr. Warrilow who was a Roman Catholic Priest, whilst he was in the theatre. Barrington was sent to London on another charge, but acquitted. (Mackenzie 1827)

Occasionally events got out of hand, particularly when drink was involved and the perpetrators of the crime appeared to receive a light sentence.

Sunday, 22nd February, 1789 – Death!

A whitesmith, John Elliott insulted tailor, Thomas Atkinson in a public house. Elliott worked with 'white' or light metals such as tin and pewter. He would have filed, polished or galvanised the metal mainly when it was cold, whereas a blacksmith works with hot metal. A fight ensued and Elliott later died of his injuries. Tried at the assizes for manslaughter, Atkinson was fined 6s. 8d. and discharged. (Mackenzie 1827)

Left: One of the many public houses in Newcastle – The Forth Tavern, near the West Wall in the mid 1800s.

15th November, 1789 – Mangled Body!

A woman's mangled body was found in Stepney Lane. Two keelmen, Fletcher Reynoldson and Robert Grey were accused of the crime and confessed. However, they each accused the other of the actual deed and were acquitted at the assizes. (Mackenzie 1827)

Punishments

The north east has a particularly bloody history between 1286 and 1550. The border area, The Marches, was a battleground between warring factions involved in blood feuds and robbery. Cumberland, Northumberland and Durham (the English Border Marches) and the Scottish Border Marches running from the north east coast to the River Cree were dangerous places to live.

Reiver bands, often a mixture of men from all social classes and both sides of the border, lived an almost nomadic, lawless existence of hit and run raiding which was to make The English Marches, basically England's buffer against Scotland, a killing zone in which both sides had to endure centuries of reiving.

Reivers wore steel bonnets like a bowl (later a burgonet with a peak), a shirt, a mail coat (the quilted leather jack or coat complete with horn or metal was more common), leather breeches and boots. They were mounted on small horses called hobblers or hobbys and murdered, raided, thieved, tracked and ambushed their way through autumn, winter and spring, when daylight was short and the nights long.

Those caught were sometimes hanged which cost money; drowned which didn't or killed in a

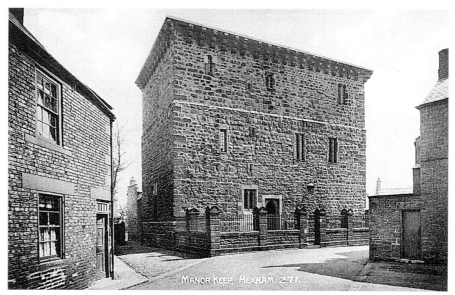

The Old Gaol, Hexham, is the first recorded purpose built prison. It was built in 1333 in Border Reiver country. Imagine how it would have felt to be a Reiver imprisoned here. Now the home of the Border History Museum.

cut and thrust fight. Towards the end of the reivers' reign one troublesome family of Grahams consisting of over a 100 people had their lands confiscated and were placed on the list for transportation on the 17th April, 1605. Some were sent to the Low Countries to serve in the British army and one group was transported to Ireland. However, many appear to have returned to the north. In Northern England and Western Scotland there is an odd surname, Maharg, which is Graham when read backwards. Is crime worse today? Was there ever a halcyon time of law and order? I'll leave you to judge.

Capital Punishment

The axe was used for beheading or quartering traitors. Their heads and body parts would then be placed for all to see above the city gates.

In 1298, Scottish leader William Wallace was hanged, drawn and quartered in London. One of the bridges on the Tyne displayed his right arm, and other 'undisclosed' parts were hung from the walls of Newcastle Keep.

After the Battle of Bannockburn in 1323, between the English and Scots, one of Andre de Hartlcla's quarters was on display on the walls of Newcastle. He was the first Earl of Carlisle.

The Percy family rebelled against Henry IV in 1400-1415. Parts of the body of Harry Hotspur, son of Henry Percy, Earl of Northumberland, were displayed on the walls of the castle.

When Sir Thomas Grey of Wark was executed for treason, his head was displayed over a gate in Newcastle.

The Bloody Code

This was the name given to English Legal System from the late 17th to early 19th century. Many crimes which we might regard as a fairly trivial offence today such as stealing from a rabbit warren and cutting down trees were punishable by death in the 1700s. The number of crimes which warranted death under the 'Code' rose from 40 in 1688, to 160 in 1765, to 225 in 1815. Thus the system became known as the 'Bloody Code'

There were three main reasons why the legal system was so brutal at this time. First the wealthy and powerful ensured they made laws which protected them. Secondly it was felt those who broke the law were greedy, lazy or sinful. Thirdly the punishments were meant to deter others.

Until the 1860s hangings were public spectacles. In Durham, hangings took place in front of the Crown Court. The wealthy, if accused of a crime, could afford legal representation and persuade the rich and powerful to give a character reference. The poor could not, so the Bloody Code was inherently unfair.

Durham in the early 1800s – The Bridge of Elvet.

Juries would often find the accused not guilty because they were aware many crimes had the penalty of death. Sometimes to ensure a lenient sentence was given, judges undervalued stolen goods. Though approximately 200 people were hanged each year at this time, fewer people appeared to have been hanged in England and Wales in the 18th century than previously. There were numerous alternatives to the death sentences in medieval times.

Branding

The plea of benefit of clergy dates back to the Middle Ages when the church was allowed to punish its own members. Since it was difficult to prove whether someone was associated with the church, judges had convicts who made this plea read from the Bible to prove their literacy and therefore their links to the church. (Most of the population in early times would have been illiterate, as education spread in later centuries this was obviously no longer the case). The verse usually chosen was Psalm 51 and became known as the 'neck verse' because it saved so many from hanging. The Psalm taken from the King James version of the Bible begins, 'Have mercy upon me, O God ...' and contains the line, 'Deliver me from bloodguiltiness, O God, thou God of my salvation: and my tongue shall sing aloud of thy righteousness.' This plea of benefit by clergy meant that those found guilty of certain felonies avoided the death penalty and were given a more lenient sentence, such as branding

In the 16th century serious offences such as theft from churches, burglary, highway robbery, horse-stealing, murder, pickpocketing and rape were non-clergyable. From 1669 to January 1707 thieves were branded on the cheek, but this meant that no one wanted to employ them, so branding reverted to the thumb.

By 1706 the reading of a text was abolished and anyone accused of an offence which had not been excluded from this privilege was allowed to plead benefit of clergy. They would have been branded on the thumb: a felon with an 'F'; a thief with a 'T' and for those convicted of manslaughter an 'M'. This was conducted after sessions in public in courtrooms. The executioner was possibly bribed to use a cold branding iron by some convicted of petty theft. Branding was an attempt to ensure that benefit of clergy could only be used once. It's interesting to note that between 1706-1718 some convicts using this plea were sentenced to hard labour in a house of correction for up to two years. The Transportation Act in 1718 meant that those who pleaded benefit of clergy could be sentenced to transportation.

There were concerns over the growth of property theft in the 17th and 18th centuries and that some offenders were receiving 'light' sentences. Offences such as cattle and sheep stealing; shop lifting property worth more than 5 shillings; house breaking and theft of 40 shillings worth of goods became non-clergyable. This meant the convict was no longer able to plead benefit of clergy and thus reduce his or her sentence. By 1779 the use of benefit of clergy ended and it was abolished in 1827.

Until the punishment of branding ended in 1779, it was probably used as a mark of shame, to humiliate and deter the victim as well as others. Before 1750, 18.8% crimes for larceny (theft) resulted in branding; in 1750-75, 22.4% and after 1775, 2.7%.

In 1775 in Hexham, a boy called John Currey stole some lead from a church and sold it to an adult, Isaac Newton. A shopkeeper, Joseph Richardon, when asked to weigh the lead, purchased some, but became suspicious. Currey was branded when found guilty and Newton was acquitted.

The Castle Keep and Black Gate – The Black Gate controlled access in and out of the Castle Keep and the castle was at one point the common prison of the county of Northumberland.

Mutilation

Mutilation, such as the chopping off of a leg or arm was also used to punish the offender and deter others.

Punishments Involving Public Ridicule

These meant public humiliation and shame for the victim through the use of ducking stool, pillory, scold's bridle, stocks, whip or the lesser known 'Newcastle cloak'. Some began as ancient, informal punishments in villages and then became part of the judicial system of punishment.

Ducking Stool

In some 17th century parish accounts the ducking stool is mentioned when justices wanted one repaired. There are few details about how often it was used to punish women convicted of being gossips or scolds. Tied in a seat attached to a long wooden arm, the woman would be ducked in the local river or pond. The last woman to be ducked in England was in 1809. Another woman was sentenced in 1817, but there was too little water.

The Pillory

Often on a platform, it consisted of a pole with holes for head and hands in a wooden frame. It was mostly used in cases of fraud or sexual abuse, but by the 1780s the pillory was regarded as dangerous as some felons had been killed by mobs. Disgusting objects such as rotten fruit and vegetables would be thrown at the miscreant. Sentences were often not carried out.

Most of the recorded sentences occurred after 1750 and were for women keeping a disorderly house and ill-defined forms of conspiracy. Assize judges in Durham sentenced two men to the pillory for false pretences in 1769, one man for rape in 1781 and in 1791 two rioters. In Newcastle the pillory was used four times for the offences of false pretences and fortune telling.

John 'Tricky' Hall already had a record. He'd tried to use a forged document in 1727, to obtain money from the estate of a dead gentleman from Lancashire. He was sentenced in 1733 to a number of years in Fleet Prison. Newcastle had to wait for him to be brought north and then pilloried him in 1736. He was 'severely pelted' for trying to forge a bond.

In 1755, a Northumberland man James Lawson was sentenced to stand in the pillory four times for 'pretending to tell fortunes and find lost goods'. Telling fortunes was linked to witchcraft and there was a suspicion that those who found the goods were often responsible for them having been 'lost'.

The pillory was often deployed in cities by the judiciary to repress dissenters or critics of royal decision making. For instance Henry James in Durham was pilloried for stating that George I was, 'neither protestant nor churchman … and I hope in a short time to be rid of him'. Susannah Fleming in 1758 and Jane Grey in 1766 were sentenced to stand in the pillory.

Susannah Fleming, whilst standing in the pillory at the 'White Cross, fainted and was almost strangled. Fortunately her life was saved by a sailor who carried her, half dead on his back, down a ladder.'

She wrote a letter addressed to Sir Walter Blackett's wife, petitioning London for clemency. Susannah explains that she was 'tryed for telling fortunes' and that several people spoke for her as they'd known her as having a, 'fair unblemished character' for thirty years.

Susannah goes on to complain that she was convicted 'on the Evidence of two wicked abandoned women' and 'ordered to be imprisoned for one year and to be set on the pillory once each Quarter.'

She then pleaded that she was, 'upwards of 80 years of age of a tender constitution and at present in a very bad state of health and the dread and apprehension of the pillory adds greatly to her Disorder and allows her little Hope of Recovery and should that punishment be inflicted it would most certainly put a period to her life …'

The White Cross was first noted in 1410. It stood in Newgate Street near the entrance to Friar Street. Traditionally markets were held between the White Cross and Newgate Street.

2nd August, 1766 – Forgery and Perjury

Jean Gray was convicted of forgery and perjury. She was sentenced to stand in the pillory, on Sandhill, Newcastle for one hour and then transported. (Read the rest of her story in the chapter Transportation to Africa and the Americas). Pillories were abolished in 1837.

The Stocks

Stocks were used in Anglo-Saxon times. The victim sat in them with his or her feet locked into holes in the wooden frame. Those watching would throw disgusting objects at them. Reverend Edmund Tew, rector of Boldon in County Durham and a Justice of the Peace, recorded in his *The Justicing Notebook* (1750-64) that he sentenced a drunkard to a period of time in the newly restored stocks in Boldon.

In 1816 a Wallsend parish had two stocks in the churchyard to deter people from Sabbath-breaking. In 1826 in Newcastle, a drunken joiner was placed in the stocks outside St Nicholas' Church. He had been shouting loudly during a Sunday service.

There were also wooden stocks in an iron cage in the churchyard of St Paul's Church in Jarrow prior to 1960. Stocks were used for petty offences, the felon being restrained for several

The stocks that once stood in St Paul's Churchyard, Jarrow.

hours. A local, George Proud, was put in them for a boyhood prank in 1877 though it's recorded that they were last used for punishment purposes in Britain in 1872.

Scold's Bridle or 'Branks'

A scold's bridle or 'branks' used in the 17th century can be found at the Guildhall in Newcastle. This was an instrument of torture in the form of a helmet like device with a bit attached which restrained the tongue. Used only on women, the idea was to prevent speech. A married woman in Morpeth in 1741 was ordered to wear it for using 'opprobrious language' towards several individuals including those who ordered the punishment: the bailiffs.

Whipping

In the 1700s, women were often jailed, whereas men could be whipped through the streets followed by sentencing to imprisonment and hard labour. Whipping was common and used by civilians and the military. For instance William Weston, in 1750, stole aprons and 'wall fruit' and was whipped from Westgate to Benwell the place of his crime.

In the 18th century those who thieved or robbed from houses or buildings were more likely to be executed than horse thieves and sheep-thieves. In the early 1700s, at the Quarter Sessions, half of the thieves were sent to jail for one year.

Right: A whipping stool.

The *Newcastle Courant* on 21st January, 1786 below, reported several crimes and their punishments, one of which was whipping:

Newcastle, January 1786

On Wednesday afternoon between five and six o'clock, a woman called at a house in this town, and pretended she was sent by a Gentleman to borrow a great coat, which she obtained, and has not been since heard of. It is hoped, this will be a caution to servants to prevent the like frauds.

Monday, being Christmas Guild, the Right Worshipful William Yielder, Esq: gave a sumptuous entertainment at the Mansion-house, to a great company of Gentlemen: and in the evening there was a brilliant assembly.

At the adjourned Sessions on Wednesday last, the following persons were convicted of petit larceny, and received the following sentences, viz. *Elizabeth, wife of William Hall, Mariner, ordered to be transported for seven years. Elizabeth, wife of William Thompson, Labourer, six months hard labour in the House of Correction. Francis Russell, Mariner, to be kept at hard labour in the House of Correction till this day, and then to be whipped round the Sand-hill, and from thence to Sandgate. Jane Stewart, single woman, one month's hard labour in the House of Correction.

After the business was finished Mr. Mayor, gave a grand entertainment at the Mansion-house, to the Bench, Juries, Gentlemen of the Law, and numerous company of the Burgessies.

Saturday last, four persons belonging to the notorious gang of Thieves and Shop-lifters, called the Bishop Auckland Gang, otherwise the Barlow Gang, otherwise the Gateshead-Fell-Gang, so called from several of them residing in these places, and from the numbers of them frequently rendezvousing there, were observed reconnoitring the Linen Drapers shops in this town, and traced to an alehouse in Pipewellgate, where they were apprehended and brought back to this town

The above Elizabeth Thompson, convicted last Wednesday was one of them. Walter Clarke, another of them, after examination escaped from the officer; and the other two, Jane Clark and Eleanor Murray, otherwise Gardiner, were committed for further examination ...'

*Elizabeth Hall see chapter on Transportation to Australia and the First Fleet.

Sometimes, even those sentenced to death would have this commuted to having to join the Army or Navy or to be transported. The other form of punishment which was used was prison (See chapter Prisons).

The 'Newcastle Cloak'

On a slightly lighter note wherever there is alcohol there have always been drunks, but have you heard of the 17th century punishment wryly called the 'Newcastle Cloak'? A drunkard would be placed in a large barrel with a hole at one end and the bottom cut out. The victim was led through the streets of Newcastle wearing his 'cloak' and no doubt being jeered at by the crowds following his progress. In the early 1700s, at the Quarter Sessions, half of the thieves were sent to jail for one year. Men convicted of a serious crime in the 18th and 19th centuries could be hanged, drawn and quartered. It was thought improper for women to be drawn and quartered. They were hanged then burnt often whilst still alive.

The local pub for Newcastle criminals was 'The Three Bulls Heads' in 'Castle Garth' which used to be beside the archway of the railway viaduct. This Public House had the worst reputation in Newcastle for its criminal clientele, made up of murderers and prostitutes.

Prisons

The Castle Keep

The Keep played a key role in local justice. In 1174 King William the Lion of Scotland was imprisoned in Newcastle for attempting to take back his lands in Northumbria which had been seized by Henry II king of England.

Interestingly William's father was Henry Earl of Northumberland. After William's capture by the English he was forced to accept Henry II as overlord of Scotland, but on Henry's death he paid 10,000 marks to Richard I of England and bought back Scotland's sovereignty,

The castle yard was used by some criminals in the 1400s as a sanctuary. The castle was part of Northumberland and outside the jurisdiction of Newcastle.

Prisoners were shackled to the wall of a keep which was susceptible to flooding, open to the elements and freezing. The inmates were not fed or given water. They were overcrowded, not segregated and there were no toilets.

There were harsh sentences for prisoners kept here such as: transportation, death by hanging, whipping and on Assizes (the county court) Sunday for the price of sixpence, the public could view and ridicule them.

The guard room of the Castle of Newcastle in 1826.

St Nicholas' Church

The western entrance to St Nicholas' Church, Newcastle, 1845.

Its 'Thief and Reiver Bell' rang to signal the beginning of the festival of St Luke and Lammas on 20th March and 12th August, offering immunity to criminals entering Newcastle. It has been a court house (Assizes Court) sentencing some prisoners to the death penalty.

In 1644 the Scots besieged Newcastle and threatened to destroy St Nicholas' steeple unless the keys of the town were given to them. Scots prisoners were bundled into the steeple by order of the mayor who said, 'our enemies shall either preserve it, or be buried in it.' The steeple was not destroyed.

The King's Justices or judges on arriving in Gateshead for Assize Week, would visit here for charitable reasons: to raise money for Newcastle Infirmary, before visiting the Newgate Street Inns.

Westgate

There is a report which states that West Gate was used to incarcerate 'unruly apprentices' and that it was also used for prisoners captured during the English Civil War 1641-1651. Some escaped apparently.

The Moot Hall

The Moot Hall in Newcastle was built In 1810. 'Moot' means meeting. The County Court and Assizes (French for 'sitting') and sometimes the Quarter Assizes (Crown Court) were held here.

County prisoners were held on the ground floor before going to Morpeth Gaol. Most of the work undertaken by the Moot Hall has been handed over to Newcastle Crown Court on the Quayside.

Right: The Moot Hall.

The Guildhall

The Assizes Court, Borough Sessions, Quarter Sessions and Assizes Week in conjunction with the Moot Hall, were held here.

Those who committed more serious crimes were tried in this building and if convicted sentenced to transportation to the Americas or Australia.

18th Century Gaols

By the 18th century gaols were basically controlled by local magistrates. Gaolers were salaried and there were fewer common abuses of prisoners. Imprisonment was not really an arduous punishment as all prisoners were required to do was not escape.

The old entrance to Durham Gaol below Elvet Bridge.

Surgeons could be called to administer to the body and ministers (ordinaries), paid for by the authorities preached and prayed for the soul. Gaols tended to be more organised and moral than a house of correction. The main difficulties may have been prisoners who were lousy, posing a threat to health or those who at the time were thought to be 'mad'.

Prisoners were allowed to complain to the local magistrates at quarter session hearings. Resident gentry or those passing through would often give charitable gifts to prisoners to ease their circumstances. Two MPs from Northumberland gave two guineas to petitioners in Durham gaol; the MP for Newcastle Sir William Blackett, ensured Newgate was supplied with coal from his mines and Quakers not only gave funding, but visited gaols.

On occasions such as Candlemas on the 2nd February, the feast of the Purification of the Blessed Virgin Mary, public celebrations were allowed in gaols.

Durham Gaol, The County Gaol, Saddler Street

The Bishop of Durham owned the County Gaol. In the early 15th century the gaol was rebuilt in Saddler Street and enlarged in 1773.

Durham Gaol housed debtors (who owed money and wouldn't be released till the sum was paid). They were held in different rooms to others who were imprisoned. Felons (those waiting trial) were here and convicted prisoners awaiting execution or transportation.

The details of prisoners below were taken from several calendars of prisoners held in northern gaols:

A CALENDAR of Prisoners in the Gaols of DURHAM, NEWCASTLE, and MORPETH, who are to take their Trials at the Assizes, 1794
PRISONERS IN DURHAM GAOL
ROBERT LISTER, late of Sherrburn, charged on suspicion of stealing a certain Black Gelding, belonging to John Watson, of Stakeford, in the parish of Beddington, in a certain field of his farm at Stakeford, in the night of the 17th October last. – Committed the 26th October, 1793, by the Rev. W. Nestfield. – To be transported for life.
JOHN HARRISON, of Easington, shoemaker, for uttering treasonable and seditious words, in the house of C. Harris, at Easington, publican. Committed the 5 November, 1793 by the Rev. Dr. Pye. On Bail. – No bill.
JOSEPH ROCHESTER, for having on the 7th January Last, made an assault on Isabella Nelson, of Sunderland, spinster, and her, (against her will) then ravished. – Acquitted.
SARAH WALTON, of Sunderland, on suspicion of picking the pocket of W. Sharp, of Kendal in Westmorland, yeoman, of his Pocket Book, containing several Bills and Parcels and other Papers. – Committed 17th March, 1794, by J. Thornhill, Esq. – No bill.
THOMAS REED, of Usworth, pit-man, charged for striking with a Bed-rail, J. Lister, late of Whickham, in an affray at Usworth, on the 14th July last; in which the said Jos. Lister received several blows from divers persons unknown, as well as from the said Thomas Reed, whereof he languished till the morning of the 16th of the same month, when he died. – Committed the 22nd July, 1794. By Henry Ellison Esq – Acquitted.

The County Gaol stood in Saddler Street, Durham. Note the austere facade. It was built to dominate the landscape and acted as a visual reminder to the population of the punishment that awaited them if they acted outside the law.

Conditions in prisons were appalling before the Gaol Act of 1823. In Durham Gaol the warder had to pay the authorities for the right to be in charge of it. Once in post, he charged the felons for basics such as food, ale, drinking water, straw for bedding and even for releasing prisoners. Unbelievably, Bainbridge Watson, one of the warders, sold alcohol which prisoners drank in a pub-like section of the gaol.

The building had three stories. The ground floor consisted of three rooms. One was a day room from which the prisoners were taken to beat hemp. The County paid each prisoner 3d a day and no deductions were made from their earnings. Prisoners were able to buy food from traders who came to the prison, but there was no provision made for their spiritual needs. In his 1803 inspection, Neild discovered activities such as picking oakum (loose hemp or jute obtained by unplaiting old ropes), spinning and picking flax (also called linseed and used for thread or in linen), but in later inspections there was no evidence of this.

In 1776 debtors were fed water soup (bread boiled in water) and whatever came into the prison from charitable donations. Debtors even appealed to Parliament complaining they were starving and in rags. Felons' rations were one pound of bread per day.

At least male and female prisoners were separated. However, at night felons were put into underground dungeons which had poor lighting and ventilation. Described by Neild as the 'worst cells in the country', the prisoners all lived and slept in this foul place.

Cells were overcrowded; waste and rubbish weren't disposed of very often and there were no sewers. Insects and bugs would have infested straw bedding and the filth would have encouraged rats. New, ill or weak prisoners would have possessions stolen and sold for water and food.

Prisoners convicted of capital offences slept in cells which were 'totally dark'. One was 19' 5'' by 13' 9'', and 9' high, the other 14' 2'' by 13' 3'', and 14' high and the floors were laid with flagstone. The cells were described by Neild in 'The Gentleman's Magazine' of 1805 as being, 'fitter for the reception of coals than any human being'.

There were numerous attempts to escape, but if caught all the prisoners were clamped in irons. This was probably because gaolers faced penalties if anyone escaped and were allowed to charge prisoners when the irons were removed.

Morpeth Gaol, New Bridge Street

Two men sent from Morpeth Gaol in 1756 to Hexham to flog Thomas Whitaker, were met by a furious crowd who jostled them so much that the flogging had to stop.

In 1777 when new laws were passed which helped debtors, prisoners 'lit up windows' set fire to tar barrels, fired guns and drank to the King and Queen.

Morpeth Court House.

A typical menu for Class 2 prisoners in 1865 is below:

PRISONERS CONFINED FOR ANY TERM EXCEEDING FOURTEEN DAYS AND NOT MORE THAN ONE CALENDAR MONTH

Meals	Males	Females
Breakfast:	1 pint of oatmeal gruel 6 ounces of bread	1 pint of oatmeal gruel 6 ounces of bread.
Dinner:	12 ounces of bread	8 ounces of bread
Supper	Same as breakfast	Same as breakfast

Prisoners of this class to have 1 pint of a soup per week.

Newgate/ Newcastle Gaol

Newgate was Newcastle's gaol from 1400 when the town became a county and was responsible for its own prisoners. A guardhouse was attached to the west wing and there was a footway on the east side through the town walls. Opposite the east end was the gaoler's house. Newgate was used for town prisoners before it was demolished in 1823 and Newcastle Great Prison was built.

Right: Newgate was heavily fortified to keep prisoners in and would be rescuers out.

Newcastle Great Prison/ the Borough Gaol, Carliol Square

Newcastle Gaol in 1826.

Designed and built by John Dobson in 1823-1828 at a cost of £35,000, it was an enormous sum for the time. The prison was in use until 1924.

Its stone walls were 25 feet high with four cell blocks built around a central tower which was the guard room. The prisoners had little privacy as the guards could see everything. There were male and female inmates.

Convicted criminals Mary Shervin, Thomas Burdis and Clement Augustin Coyle will all have spent time in this gaol.

Mary Shervin aged only 21 from Alnwick was only 4' 10'', single, with brown hair. However, she had two aliases Sharon or Sheridan when she was arrested for stealing money on 20th March, 1873 in Newcastle. She was sentenced to one calendar month in prison with Hard Labour.

Executioners were often the public hangman and inexperienced in beheading. Execution by beheading was rare, usually for treason, in public and reserved for the nobility as it was regarded as a fast and honourable death, unlike hanging which involved slow asphyxiation at this time.

25th September, 1705
The Appointment of an Executioner!

'Alexander Robinson was employed by the corporation of Newcastle to be 'common executioner in hanging felons, putting persons in the pillory, clearing the streets of swine, and to doe and perform all other matters belonging to the place and duty of 'hougher'. A 'hougher' cut the sinews of houghs of swine found in the streets and was also the executioner of felons.

One of the most infamous hangmen William Curry, otherwise known as 'Mutton Curry', was unsurprisingly a convicted sheep stealer from York. He was sentenced to death twice, but this was commuted twice to transportation to Australia. He was persuaded to take the post of hangman in about 1802. Gin was apparently his downfall. He hanged numerous criminals over 33 years, including 13 in one day in 1813. Unfortunately he bungled more than one execution.

On 14th April, 1821 Curry hanged one man in York and was supposed to hang a second, William Brown, later at Baile Hall. By the time he arrived, Curry was so drunk, he suggested the crowd tried the noose. He attempted several times to put the hood on Brown's head and then struggled with the noose. In the end he had to be assisted to hang Brown.

A few months later on 1st September, 1821, Curry had to hang 5 men together at York Castle. All went as it should, except for Curry who shot through the trapdoor at the same time as the hanged men, thankfully he didn't have a noose round his neck!

Hangman, Murdock of Glasgow executed Irishman Mark Sherwood on the 23rd August, 1844 in

Newcastle Gaol – Note the tall, severe buildings with small windows encircled by a high wall.

Newcastle Gaol for murdering his wife Ann. Sherwood had almost severed her head from her body in the previous March.

Nathan Howard of York executed Patrick Forbes in Newcastle Gaol in 1850 for the murder of his wife Elizabeth. Howard was elderly and infirm, and bungled his last hanging leaving Forbes violently writhing in his death throes at the end of the rope. Howard was dismissed and died six days later. (See Chapter The Gallows Walk for more information about Forbes.)

Thomas Askern was York's last hangman from 1856-1878 and was apparently the last hangman to hold a provincial post in Britain and followed the 'short drop' procedure. He held the post despite numerous bungled hangings in York and elsewhere. George Vass was hanged by him at Newcastle Great Prison on the 16th March, 1863.

Vass murdered an old woman, Margaret Docherty, who had been first footing on the previous New Year's Day. She lived in Buckingham Street and was married to a tailor. The doctor at the inquest, Dr. Rayne, stated that it was if a machine had mutilated her body. Vass' execution went to plan.

Winlaton miner, Matthew Atkinson was also hanged by Askern on the 16th March, 1865 at Durham. Atkinson had been drinking all day and when he returned home there was no meal prepared for him or a fire lit. He cornered his wife in a neighbour's house at Spen and killed her.

Public hangings were not what they used to be. The mob were only allowed to see the white hood put on Atkinson's head and the noose placed round his neck, because his body dropped behind a wall at the moment of execution. The crowd heard the dull thud as Atkinson hit the ground when the rope snapped! Just 30 minutes later Atkinson was hanged with a shorter and thicker rope giving him a slow, painful death as it did not break his neck. (See Chapter The Gallows Walk.)

Askern had to be smuggled out of Edinburgh in disguise after a hanging when the condemned man, with mental difficulties, struggled at the end of a rope for 4 minutes to the shocked horror of the spectators.

Lincolnshire born, William Marwood was so famous he was even the subject of children's rhyme and national pun, 'If Pa killed Ma, who'd kill Pa? Marwood.' He had business cards printed stating:

'William Marwood. Public Executioner' and a shop sign with the words 'Crown Officer'. A retired cobbler, by the time he was 54, he had hanged 176 people. The first to have a professional approach to the job, he was ironically paid at piece-rate.

Marwood had a scientific and innovative approach to the role of hangman as he was the first to put into practise the medical theory that the 'long drop', once the build of the condemned and the length of drop had been calculated, would cause instantaneous unconsciousness and death two minutes afterwards. He also introduced tables calculating the relationship between the length of drop and the victim's weight. He moved the knot to under the left ear and the drop was increased to 8-10 feet. He ensured the rope ran smoothly by specifying a metal ring instead of a slip knot and the use of a leather washer. He also apparently was the first to use the split trapdoor. Before this the condemned died of slow suffocation by hanging or were decapitated.

The basic conditions inside the prison cell were perhaps better than enjoyed by some prisoners in their own homes.

However, when Marwood hanged James Burton at Durham Gaol in 1883 he bungled the execution. Burton had entered into a bigamous marriage to an unknowing Elizabeth Sharpe in January 1883. When she discovered this, she left him. He murdered her at night close to Silksworth Colliery, Sunderland by hitting her on the head with a stone and burying her there.

When the lever was pulled on the trapdoor, and Burton dropped, the rope tangled itself around his arm and the noose went under his chin as he swung. Having untangled him, Marwood pushed him to a slow, agonising death.

The most famous and respected hangman of them all was Albert Pierrepoint, Chief Executioner for the United Kingdom from 1932-1956. He learnt the trade from his Uncle Tom. Albert's father Henry hanged 29 year old Abel Atherton at Durham on 8th December, 1909 for shooting 33 year old Elizabeth Ann Patrick.

Albert executed up to 600 people 16 of whom were women and 200 were Nazi war criminals. He was Britain's most prolific executioner.

Urban Watchmen or The Watch

A good example of use of the Watch was in Newcastle which was divided into 25 wards in the 18th century. Two constables on average were allocated to a ward, though some had four or even six. There were 60 constables in the 1730s who appear to have recruited inhabitants of Newcastle to be watchers, who were to meet at the porch of St Nicholas' every night at eight 'with arms well provided'. If they refused they had to pay a fine. However, some houses were allowed to 'watch for themselves'. Guilds and other groups also seem to have contributed regular members. Surprisingly, women could also participate if they ran a business. Groups of 40 or 50 during the day and up to 90 at night were made up of colliers, weavers, hostmen and merchants.

A member of one of the wealthier trades, appointed with a salary by the Common Council and the constables in each ward, supervised the watching system. They were probably excused night duty, unlike some constables, if there were sufficient watchmen. Extra patrols and special look-outs were ordered if a serious crime had been committed.

Old Houses at the head of the Long Stairs, Castle Garth in Newcastle in the early 1800s. Imagine having to keep watch in areas like this.

Constables and watchmen were often assaulted and in one case killed. Newcastle's urban watch system came fairly close to providing a police service somewhat similar to that of today.

The records strongly suggest that most constables worked hard to find stolen property, thieves and murderers. However, Thomas Tate, the Newcastle turnkey, unfortunately, stands out for all the wrong reasons. He was found to be a burglar when he gave stolen cloth to his godchild. When arrested, he boasted he'd break out of jail in less than fifteen minutes, which he did by unlocking his chains. He was given a permanent guard, found guilty of petty larceny and transported.

Left: Back yards and back lanes in North Shields before the Second World War. Two hundred years after the formation of the Watch, areas like this were still tough areas for the police of the twentieth century.

The Police Force

Being a police officer has always been a dangerous job. Records show that many a 'bobby' drowned, tripped or fell in suspicious circumstances.

Policing, started in Newcastle in 1763 when the Northumberland and Lighting Watch Commission patrolled the walls. Officer William Atkinson from Newcastle, was trying to arrest someone and was killed with an axe in June 1756.

Until 1812 the Watch's authority was restricted to within Newcastle's walls, after this date when lighting became more popular, patrols began outside Newcastle walls.

It was left to individuals to form groups, advertise, glean information, detain suspects, take them to a parish constable, then a magistrate and finally gaol to await trial. The parish constable would have been an unpaid local volunteer and an Act of Parliament in 1873 stopped their appointments. You needed money and position to create groups of like-minded men and receive some sort of justice; what justice was there for the poor, unless they had a benefactor?

The first recorded suggestion anywhere of 'police' was to do with Stockton and Darlington Railway employees on the 30th June, 1826. However, the word 'constable' wasn't used and they may just have been in charge of the trains.

A professional full time police force was needed for the rest of the nation. Despite strong opposition, Sir Robert Peel, the Home Secretary created the Metropolitan Police (Metropolitan Police Act 1829) and the seeds of our modern police force.

Andrew Findlay, formerly a sergeant, in the uniform of a Superintendent of Newcastle City Police. He retired from the police on the 19th December, 1904.

It wasn't until the 1830s that police forces, as we know them, were established in places like London. Railway police forces had been formed in certain areas at this time. Unfortunately the first attempt to create a police force in Newcastle with 8 constables from November 1832 to September 1833 was a disaster and only lasted a year. The public didn't appear to like the experience. It wasn't till 1835 that a permanent, professional police force, the Newcastle Borough Police led by Superintendent John Stephens and controlled by the Watch Committee was established. By 1868 telegraph was used to communicate between police stations.

The police office and the Hospital of the Holy Jesus, Manors, Newcastle in 1845.

By 1871 the Newcastle police had its headquarters at Manors, built by John Dobson near the town gaol in Carliol Square. Apart from cells for holding prisoners, the building also incorporated Manors Police Court which replaced the Guildhall.

At this time the police force consisted of 173 constables and was short staffed. Unmarried men were housed in barracks and those with wives or families lived in designated houses or flats. Several police stations were built, one in an old hospital on Westgate Road; others at Laurel Street at Elswick, the Ouseburn and Prudoe Street.

The Municipal Corporations Act 1835 allowed Boroughs to have their own Police Forces. Durham City Police was formed in February 1836 and Gateshead Borough Police in October 1836. There is a record of Gateshead PC Graham who was 27 years old and died in a warehouse explosion when assisting at a fire.

Sunderland Borough Police was created in 1837. Sergeant John Hacker was killed with a Borough PC in November 1895, aged 47, at the scene of a fire when the roof collapsed.

South Shields Borough Police was established in 1839. PC Thomas Rodgers is recorded as being drowned at sea whilst on duty on 21st May, 1914, he was 34 years old.

The origins of the River Tyne Police lie with the 'Serjeants of the Water' and 'Water Baliffs' who worked for Newcastle's Corporation.

An early policebox in South Shields.

Established in 1845, the River Tyne Police was a separate force and patrolled on and around the Tyne protecting lives, property and upholding law and order under the Corporation's Watch Committee. The Force worked under the authority of the Tyne Improvement Committee (TIC). Their police stations were in Gateshead, Newcastle, North and South Shields and Walker.

Handy notes from 1920.

The River Police handled incidents such as dangerous land and ship fires; murders, shipwrecks and so on. Their mode of transport was steam and motor launches. It was obviously a dangerous job as Sub Inspector Richard Pickering, aged 51, was killed when a tug crashed into his boat on the 6th January, 1873.

By 1852 the River Tyne Police were being administered by the Improvement Commissioners and the Superintendents of River Police till 1968 and in 1974 it became part of Northumbria Police.

The TIC's Docks and Piers Police Service was created in the 1870s. A Sergeant John Anthony, aged 47, is recorded as having been hit by a locomotive and died of his injuries in March, 1922. This Service had less status than the River Police, and ceased to exist in 1949.

Walker Police Station shortly after opening.

The Gallows Walk

Executions in Newcastle

A typical gallows could be the nearest tree or a raised platform about 10' square. Made of rough planks, it would have a railing on all sides and on the day of execution it was draped in black. If the punishment was beheading, straw would be scattered on the boards to soak up the blood. The oak block stood in a basket of sawdust ready for the severed head.

What followed was real theatre. It was expected that the prisoner climbed steps to the 'stage' and showed courage whilst making a dignified speech. They then knelt. A blindfold was offered so that the prisoner wouldn't see the axe and turn at the last moment. The vertebrae and neck muscles are tough and all prisoners feared it could take more than one strike of the axe. Once the head was struck off the executioner would hold it aloft and cry, 'Behold the head of a traitor!'

The Tyne Bridge stands on the site of Sandhill. The area was the centre of Medieval Newcastle where markets, plays, bull baiting and executions took place.

25th January, 1768 – Bullish Behaviour

'a sailor was killed by a bull, which the populace were baiting on the Sandhill, Newcastle.' (Mackenzie 1827)

A head on display in Newcastle.

There is no longer a hill, but there seven ancient houses remain, Bessy Surtees' being one, which give us a flavour of the time.

One of the most ancient sites for hangings in Newcastle was the Town Moor. It's a large grassy area situated to the north of Newcastle and is now owned by Newcastle City Council and the Freemen of the city.

From 1400 Newgate Gaol housed condemned prisoners who would have walked along Gallowgate Road (to the left of Andrew Tower and Newgate) to a tree which acted as a gallows in Gallows Hole at the entrance to the Town Moor. These processions would have drawn crowds who flocked to see the 'show' at the end of the walk.

Between 1650-1829, more than forty people died on these gallows with crowds of 20,000 gathering to watch the procession and the hanging. Witches were hanged here.

Identifying witches was highly lucrative for a witch-finder. Before the Enlightenment, superstition and not scientific fact was the basis for a judgement of death for witchcraft. The first woman hanged in England for being a witch was Agnes Waterhouse from Chelmsford in Essex and Newcastle had its very own witch trials.

Left: Sandhill, Newcastle in 1826.

Witch Trials!

In 1650, thirty women were accused of being witches and dancing with the devil. It's possible that the witch hunt was led by Scottish witch-finder Cuthbert Nicholson. He'd have been paid 20 shillings (£1) for each witch he discovered. A suspect's skin was pricked with a blunt pin perhaps, or in a wart which did not bleed and this was taken as proof of guilt.

On 21st August, 1650 one man and sixteen women were hanged on the Town Moor in Newcastle as witches: Mathew Boulmer, Isabell Brown, Margrit Brown, Elsabeth Anderson, Elsabeth Dobson, Ellenor Henderson, Aylles Hume, Jane Hunter, Jane Koupling, Margrit Maddeson Jane Martin, the miller's wife, Margrit Moffet, Marie Pootes Ellenor Robson, Ellenor Rogers, Ann Watson and Katren Welsh.

In Durham Nicholson exposed two women as witches and in Northumberland he was paid £3 per witch. He later confessed to being responsible for the deaths of 220 women and was executed in Scotland for trickery.

The last woman executed for being a witch in England was Alice Mulholland who was hanged in Exeter in 1686.

Murder commanded the death sentence until the late 20th century and this was the case for keelman Richard Brown. Living in the tight knit community of Sandgate in the 18th century, Brown would have laboured on a keel, a small, square, bucket-shaped, flat-bottomed, square shaped boat. A keel could carry 2.15 tonnes of coal. It usually had a five man crew, but if the tide was against them, women would pull the keels to the waiting colliers on the Tyne. A keelman's job involved hard physical effort and few could continue in this employment beyond forty.

A lot of people would have known and worked with Brown who was executed on the Town Moor for the murder of his daughter.

A hanging on the Town Moor, Newcastle.

There were many craftsman in Newcastle, but perhaps none envisaged their end at the hands of a soldier. Robert Parker was a cooper. The term 'cooper' may originally have come from Latin for 'vat' and Middle Dutch 'kupe' meaning a basket, tub or wood. Being a cooper meant you were a craftsman and would have made wooden barrels, butts, butter churns, casks and so on.

27th September, 1752 – Cooper Murder!

Just several years after the Scottish rebellion in 1745, a Scots accent was probably not too popular in Newcastle. After a brawl in the Bigg Market, Robert Parker was stabbed in the throat by Ewan Macdonald, a recruit in General Guises' army. Sentenced to death, Macdonald hurled the hangman off the ladder resting on the scaffold.

Macdonald was restrained and executed on the Town Moor, but showed signs of life on the surgeon's slab. He was finished off with a mallet and his body later dissected and anatomized in the Surgeon's Hall. 'The young man had been grossly irritated to the perpetration of his crime, though not by the person that was killed.'

Perhaps Parker worked at The Cooperage, on Newcastle Quayside, a 13th century merchant's house which became a cooper's workshop in the 18th century. He would never have imagined his end, nor would Macdonald, though throughout history human cadavers have been dissected by doctors, legally or illegally, to inform them about the internal workings of the human body. The Murder Act of 1752 stated that bodies of executed murderers could be dissected and anatomized. This meant preserved parts of the body would be put on display for the education of the medical fraternity.

The Scotch Inn, Bigg Market, Newcastle in the 17th century.

The original Barber Surgeon's Hall in Newcastle was built in the 1640s and was used for teaching medicine. A round dissection table was surrounded by benches. Behind these were specimens in the shape of skeletons and bodies held together by wire. Upstairs, visitors were apparently offered the opportunity to touch a stuffed skin in human form. The original surgeon's Hall was demolished because of the building of the North Shields and Berwick railway.

Between the years 1735 and 1799, 6,069 males and 375 females were hanged in England and Wales.

7th August, 1758 – Woman Hanged!

'At the assizes this year, Alice Williamson, was condemned for burglary, and executed on the Town Moor.' (Mackenzie 1827)

Frances Kidder was the last woman publicly hanged in Britain on 2nd April, 1868 at Maidstone and 28 year old Ruth Ellis, who shot her lover David Blakely, was the last woman to suffer the death penalty in Britain on the 13th July, 1955.

Left: Ruth Ellis – the last women to executed in Britain.

In a fight between a pawn-broker and a keelman, you'd expect the tough keelman to win, but this wasn't case in the incident between George Stewart and Robert Lindsay. Known by their sign of three golden balls, pawn-brokers have lent money for hundreds of years in exchange for goods of similar value. Property was redeemed by paying back the loan with interest.

27th August, 1764 – Shooting!

Pawn-broker, Stewart, shot Lindsay, a keelman. Stewart, from Sandgate, was executed on the Town Moor. Sandgate was a district as well as a street. Situated close to the Tyne, it was densely populated. Keelmen were mainly housed in the narrow lanes.

From 2004 to 2010, 1,842 postmen have been convicted for stealing post. One postman, recently stole £4,000 in postal surcharge fees and received 200 hours community service as a punishment. Compare this to the case of Robert Knowles in 1776.

21st August, 1776 – Stealing a Letter!

A North Shields postman, Knowles stole a letter containing two £50 Bank of England bills from Newcastle Post Office. They belonged to Newcastle merchant, Robert Rankin. His employer, the Postmaster, could have been an innkeeper as they found stabling for the postboys and horses in the 17th and 18th centuries. It was later felt that inns weren't the most secure places for mailbags, unfortunately neither were Post Offices. Knowles was executed on Newcastle Town Moor for his crime.

Condemned prisoners often made a speech at the gallows. If they were brave they would entertain the crowds by joking and poking fun at the hangman.

17th November, 1783 – Forgery!

William Alexander was convicted, 'for the forgery of a bill of exchange', supposedly written by 'Samuel Jenkinson, of New York, on Messrs, Grey and Ogilvie, London.' Alexander apparently, 'died with great firmness and decency. His Meditations, Letters and Speech at the place of execution, were afterwards printed.' He came to Newcastle in the preceding month of April, under the name of George Ross, surgeon of his majesty's ship *Resolution*. He had several aliases such as William Alexander, George Ross and George Christie. He was executed on the Town Moor, Newcastle and is buried in St Andrew's churchyard.

Right: The tower of St Andrew's Church, Newcastle, 1845.

Footpads robbed people on the street, but were on foot, unlike highwaymen who were on horseback. The punishment for footpads was usually imprisonment or transportation, some were not so fortunate.

26th August, 1784 – Robbery!

William Collins and James Chambers were seamen. They were convicted of robbing Mr Jasper Anderson of Coxlodge, close to his home. They were executed on the Town Moor in Newcastle. However, the sentence of capital punishment was not just given for robbery.

30th August, 1786 – Horse Stealing!

Horse stealing was rife in the north east. Henry Jennings was convicted as a horse thief. Before Jennings' execution on Newcastle's Town Moor and whilst he was standing at the gallows, he read out examples of 'cant' which he wanted to be published to help the public.

Cant was the peculiar language or slang used by the 18th century underworld. Examples of 18th century cant are: a 'keffal' or 'prancer' which was a horse; a 'queere prancer' an ordinary cheap horse or cowardly horse-stealer and a 'rum-prancer' a fine horse.

Westgate

Named after one of the gates in the city wall, it is situated to the west of the city. Early in the history of Newcastle, those sentenced to be hanged, were kept for two days in the Castle Keep's dungeon and then taken in procession past Baliff's Gate, Black Gate and along Westgate Road to be executed. Before 1752 County prisoners convicted at the County Assizes were hanged at the public gallows in Bath Lane.

Sentenced at the County Assizes, John Wilson and Michael Curry were executed at Westgate on the 4th September, 1739 for murder. Wilson murdered Barbara Tremble and Curry murdered Robert Shearvel.

In 1752 a new gallows was built outside Westgate, near the Tyne Theatre. A number of executions took place here.

Right: The Chapel of the Hospital of St Marie, Westgate, Newcastle.

3rd September, 1764 – Breaking and Entering

'James Edgar was executed, at the Westgate, for breaking into the house of Edward Bigge, Esq. of West Jesmond.' (Mackenzie 1827)

Highway robbery was very common in the 18th century. There were not many banks and people carried their money with them. Roads were bad, travel slow and there was no police force.

21st August, 1776 – Highway Robbery!

A soldier, Andrew Mackenzie, was executed at Westgate for highway robbery.

A gang of three heartless rogues, two women and a man met gruesome ends at Westgate.

10th August, 1792 – Crozer killing!

Eleanor Clark, Jane Clark and William Winter were convicted of murdering an elderly woman, Margaret Crozer at Elsden, Northumberland. They were all executed at Westgate, Newcastle.

Winter's body was suspended in chains on Whiskershields Common, but the bodies of the two women were dissected at the Surgeon's Hall and then buried.

Some Executions in Newcastle Gaol:

30th August, 1850 – Murder of Wife!

Elizabeth Forbes was murdered by her husband Patrick Forbes, an Irish labourer on 30th August, 1850. They lived at Cloggers Entry at the head of the Side and had been drinking in Robertson's spirits shop. The Side was a place where people had lived and shopped since medieval times. It was situated beside the castle. Two neighbours helped Elizabeth to climb the stairs. That night the married couple slept in the same bed as their son Thomas. Bridget, their daughter had been in several times with bread for Thomas. The following day, Elizabeth was found lying in her own blood.

A passing policeman heard Bridget cry, 'Murder!' No visible wounds could be found on the body, but the inquest found that knives in Patrick's pocket could have caused wounds. In his last official statement on 23rd August, 1850 Forbes said, 'I loved my wife sincerely … I was very drunk and am not conscious of myself having done anything to cause the death of my dear wife: but believing the deed not done by any other person I am willing to take the blame of it upon myself …'

His execution by hanging was witnessed by a large crowd of mainly men who behaved as if it was a public holiday. The hangman was 74 year old Howard of York.

A reporter from the *Newcastle Chronicle* heard Forbes say repeatedly, 'O Lord Jesus' and 'Saints pray for me'. He had to be supported on to the drop and trembled as he said, 'Mercy Jesus' while a cap was placed over his head; the rope with its knot put in the correct position and the ankle restraints tied. With hands as if in prayer, the bolt for the drop was drawn. Unfortunately the first attempt to hang Forbes was botched as he fell partly on and under the scaffold. The second attempt was instantly successful. He was buried in the prison grounds.

'Beside' the castle, the Side is medieval in origin. People lived, shopped and travelled through here. It was one of two streets (the other being Pilgrim Street) leading towards and away from the one bridge on the Quayside.

14th March, 1863 – Last Public Hanging at Newcastle Gaol

George Vass was the last person publicly hanged here. (See Chapter The Enforcers)

23rd December, 1875 – Last Private Hanging at Borough Gaol!

John William Anderson was hanged in Newcastle Gaol in private for the murder of his wife. It seems likely he was hanged by William Marwood from Horncastle, Lincolnshire, who devised the more humane method of execution of the 'long drop'. The neck was broken instantly and the prisoner died of asphyxia whilst unconscious as opposed to the 'short drop' and slow strangulation.

Those convicted at the Newcastle City Assizes were taken to Fair Moor, Morpeth to be hanged, a journey of over 2 days, 2-3 weeks after conviction. On the 17th August, 1742 there were two hangings: William Simpson for horse theft and John Todd for sheep stealing.

The Last Public Execution in Durham Gaol

Matthew Atkinson was the last person publicly executed on the 16th March, 1865.

1873 – Mary Ann Cotton – Serial Murderer!

The judge, placed a black cap on his head and concluded by passing sentence on Mary Ann Cotton in the usual words: 'In these words shall I address you, I would earnestly urge you to seek for your soul that only refuge which is left to you, in the mercy of God through the atonement of our Lord, Jesus Christ. It only remains for me to pass upon you the sentence of the law, which is that you will be taken hence to the place from whence is that you came, and from thence to a place of execution, and there to be hanged by the neck until you are dead, and your body be afterwards buried within the precincts of the gaol. And may the Lord have mercy on your soul.'

Mary Ann Cotton, Britain's most notorious female serial killer was executed at the age of 40 on the 24th March, 1873 in Durham Prison for the murder of her nephew, Charles Cotton but twenty one people who had known her well had died; many probably from arsenic poisoning.

Her maiden name was Robson and she was born in Murton, near Seaham, County Durham, in 1832 to a pitman father who was killed when Mary was 14. She was an apprentice dress maker at 16, but married a timekeeper, William Mowbray when she was 20. They moved to Devon where they had five children. Four were dead by the time the Mowbrays returned to County Durham. They eventually settled in Sunderland and had three more children who died as did their father. Mary received £35 worth of insurance money.

Sunderland High Street in the 1880s.

Whilst working as a nurse at Sunderland Infirmary, she married a patient, George Ward. He was an engineer and died over a year later. James Robinson a shipyard foreman, widower and father of young children, advertised for a housekeeper. He employed Mary a month after her husband's death. Within a week, Robinson's ten month old son was dead. The death was recorded as gastric fever. Then there were more deaths. In 1867 Mary's remaining child, two more of Robinson's children and Mary's mother died.

However, Robinson married Mary and they had two more children together, one of whom died before it was a year old. Mary's spending got the family into debt causing arguments. The marriage was in trouble. Mary suggested her husband take out life assurance, perhaps suspicious of her motives, he refused and she walked out.

Mary's sister Margaret, who died of stomach pains some time afterwards, introduced her to widower Frederick Cotton in 1870. Cotton's wife had recently died of TB and typhus had killed his two children. It is easy to see how Mary and Frederick would have had some common ground. Heavily pregnant, Mary committed bigamy (Robinson was still alive) when she married Frederick in September 1870. Within a week she took out insurance on her 'husband' and his two sons.

The famous photograph of Mary Ann Cotton.

After a year of living in West Auckland, Frederick was dead and within three months, Mary's new lover, Joseph Nattrass moved in. Needing employment, Mary found work as a nurse to an excise officer, Mr Quick-Manning who had smallpox. She started a relationship with him and within weeks Nattrass, a stepson and her son died.

Though Mary was pregnant with Quick-Manning's child, he wouldn't marry her. Desperate for money, she took in lodgers and found extra work. She was asked by an assistant overseer, Thomas Riley, if she'd nurse another smallpox patient, but refused because she said she had to look after her stepson, Charles. She asked if Charles could go in the workhouse without her, adding something like, 'I won't be troubled long.' Charles died within a week. Riley informed the police.

A verdict of death by natural courses was recorded, but a post mortem was ordered. Tests found traces of arsenic in Charles' stomach and organs. It was probably used because it was cheap, similar to flour or sugar and couldn't be smelt or tasted. Mary was arrested and when her other victims' bodies were exhumed, arsenic was again found.

Primarily charged with the murders of Charles Cotton, Joseph Nattrass, Frederick Cotton and Robert Ranson Cotton, Mary was only tried for the murder of her stepson, Charles. Despite pleading her innocence, on 8th March, 1873 she was found guilty and sentenced to death.

She'd all ready given birth to a girl in January and there was no reason for the sentence not to be carried out. She was hanged by William Walcraft in Durham Prison on 24th March, 1873 and is remembered in a macabre nursery rhyme:

'Mary Ann Cotton.

She's dead and she's rotten

She lies in her bed,

Her eyes wide open

Sing, sing, oh what can I sing,

Mary Cotton is tied up with string

Where, where? Up in the air

Selli' black puddens a penny a pair.'

The Last Private Execution at Durham Gaol

Private Brian Chandler was executed on the 17th December, 1958 by the hangman Robert Stewart and his assistant Tommy Cunliffe. Chandler's victim was 83 year old Martha Dodd who he battered to death. The jury deliberated for about one and a half hours before coming to the conclusion that Chandler had stolen from Mrs Dodd. This made it a capital crime under the 1957 Homicide Act.

Transportation to Africa and the Americas 1616-1776

Until 1660 the punishment for treason or a felony, with one exception was death. The exception was petty larceny for which whipping was the sentence. Many were saved from the death penalty by pleading 'benefit of clergy' or receiving a royal pardon.

In the 17th century transportation was seen as a more humane punishment than death. Some convicts went to West Africa, though over a period of 160 years most were sent to the Americas and later Australia which was a penal colony for 80 years. About 1,200 people involved in political or social unrest were also transported.

In the early 18th century the prosecution of criminals in England was usually carried out by the victim. Filing charges and presenting evidence were all down to him. Constables were not paid unless the victim did so. The courts let someone go, if innocent; if guilty they were imprisoned or hanged.

Later in the century if the victim won, the prisoner was either hanged, transported or pardoned. Justice or revenge were the only incentives for the victim. Later large rewards were offered for convictions for serious crimes. It appears sometimes there was no offence or people were entrapped. Witnesses also expected a reward and juries were aware of this and their testimonies were often discounted.

In 1752 the reward system was replaced by a system which reimbursed prosecutors. However, this did not always work. Despite this in 1778 a prosecutor could be reimbursed for an unsuccessful prosecution. By the late 18th century, most prosecutions were private, but the private prosecutor would have been a police officer.

The appalling conditions on board a transport ship.

Prisoners from the North Transported to the Americas in 1616-1776

In 1718 the first Transportation Act stated that convicts could be sentenced to transportation to America for 7 years. Some parts of northern England adopted this punishment simultaneously. This meant those reprieved from the death sentence or convicted of offences such as petty or grand larceny, could be transported.

Bear in mind that convict records in particular are subject to human error, deliberate 'mistakes' to conceal identity, sentences being commuted and so on, making it difficult to track some individuals.

Approximately 4,500 felons, mainly for minor offences, were transported from the northern courts, Northumberland was the exception. Horse and cattle theft was a huge problem in this county, but horse thieves who were caught were rarely executed. Private merchants were paid a subsidy of £3 per transportee. This meant they could also profit from selling him or her into indentured servitude for their convicted term. No one wanted to transport the old, diseased or infirm, but there was profit to be made out of the young and healthy.

In 1740 the Guildhall riots took place because of rising corn prices. This was apparently the worst case of civil disorder in Newcastle's history. The Assizes tried 27 men and women for attacking the Guildhall in Sandhill.

9th June, 1740

'There was a riot in Newcastle. The militia opened fire and killed one. Seven men were later transported.' (Mackenzie 1827)

There are differing reports as to the number transported to North America. Research indicates that there were six: Thomas Grey, James Harriot, Thomas Wilson, William Sopit, Robert Hatherick (alias Hatherwick) and William Keed (alias Kid, Keedy).

Once in America, few convicts appear, on the surface, to have escaped and returned to their original homes. *The Newcastle Gazette* 15th April, 1752, recorded Sandgate schoolmaster, Durham Hill, stealing books and sentenced to transportation to South Carolina for seven years. Escaping slaves, convicts and indentured servants found it difficult to avoid detection.

No distinction was made between ordinary servants and convicts. Owners privately inspected their bodies and recorded identification marks. James Wilson alias Miles Townsend from Newcastle had a tattoo of the letters MT.

Handbills, advertisements and news stories written by masters and mistresses, described the appearance, character and origins of any escapee. However, few white women were described as intimately as men.

After 1720, newspapers and criminal writings suggest a number of those transported, came back to England illegally as in the case of Jane Grey on 2nd August, 1766. Jane Grey was an innkeeper in New Bridge Street, Newcastle, who sold mutton pies. She was the wife of a pensioner. Thomas Jameson was a well known engraver, printer and Jane's lover. Jane became involved in passing forged notes with Thomas.

This shows the thriving industry on the river and Quayside as well as the prosperity the ships must have brought to Newcastle. Unfortunately it was also the point of departure for convict ships.

Jane at first claimed that Jameson had thought of the plan as he was in debt and about to become bankrupt. He'd done the engraving and printing, she said, and she'd used between ten and twelve £5 notes in her 'various businesses'. After they were both arrested and prosecuted, Grey appears to have changed her story. Jameson was acquitted and fled. Grey was convicted of forgery and perjury. She was sentenced to stand in the pillory on Sandhill for one hour and was then transported on the *Mary* from Shields to Virginia for seven years. There are reports of her selling pies on her return.

William Brown's nickname was Sir William as he often pretended to be a gentleman. He escaped from Morpeth jail in 1731 and the price of five guineas was put on his head. He was described as fair and 6 feet tall. He was caught in 1740 and sentenced at the Newcastle Assizes to transportation to America.

Forced to work on a tobacco plantation in Virginia, he escaped and returned to England. One of his gang betrayed him. Brown pleaded that a press gang had kidnapped him. He was sentenced on 8th August, 1743.

Leg irons on board a transport ship – These would have restricted the convicts' movement, probably given them leg sores and made escape almost impossible.

Monday, 8th August, 1743

'William Brown, leader of a band of thieves or Moss Troopers was convicted of returning from transportation. The execution was hastened for fear of rescue. He was hanged at Westgate, Newcastle.' (Mackenzie 1827)

One street robber, James Dalton was transported and 'returned' to England twice. He kept a record of his 'returned' friends which could be read in criminal biographies published in newspaper articles and pamphlets at the time. Requests for pardons usually featured confessions like this.

Robber John Poulter was arrested and attempted to turn King's evidence against his friends. He wrote, *The Discoveries of John Poulter alias Baxter*. It was so popular it ran to at least eight editions. He used examples of friends who had 'returned' as a guide for convicts to help them back to England. One suggestion was to transfer to a ship going to England once you were in an American harbour. Whether Dalton or Poulters' accounts can be trusted, is for you to decide. Poulter eventually escaped from jail, but was recaptured and executed.

Between 1760 and 1770 running away was common. Men, as opposed to women, escaped within two years of landing, some within two months. Advertisements offering a £3 reward from public funds for their capture were used in the Pennsylvania and Chesapeake colonies of Virginia and Maryland.

In 1768, Christopher Armstrong, a Cumberland horse and sheep thief, was transported. Harry Piper, the shipping agent in Alexandria Virginia, was warned by letter that Armstrong might be trouble. He was sold for £8 as a servant. Unfortunately,

Piper later reported to his employers that Armstrong had run away and stolen a 'fine horse'. He was never heard of again.

Samuel Gasford, transported on the *Thornton*, ran away, from the Reverend Brockes in Virginia within months. His escape was advertised in the *Maryland Gazette* 2nd October, 1772, 'It has been discovered since he ran away that this is not the first time of his being convicted to America, and that he is well acquainted with the County of Northumberland.'

Between 1718 and 1775 out of approximately 50,000 people who left the shores of England and Ireland, 43% were convicts. Some were members of well organised gangs, like the Faws who were made up of married couples, their children and partners and probably never became indentured servants.

13th April, 1752

Eighteen faws, strollers, or vagrants, from Morpeth, were shipped aboard the Owner's Goodwill, Captain Morland, lying in the Tyne, in order to be transported to South Carolina.' (Mackenzie 1827)

The *Newcastle Courant*, 18th April, 1752, recorded Northumberland magistrates sentencing William Fall and 16 of his 'gang' to transportation to South Carolina, yet at least 12 had returned within two years.

In 1763 Alderman John Hewitt arrested William Fall, alias Smith and 14 others at Coventry Fair. All bar one had returned from transportation. William and Jane Fall had a house in Northumberland described as 'a kind of garrison and the repository of the stolen property and cattle from all parts of the kingdom, brought there by the gang.' Surprisingly, in the American colonies absences of slaves and servants were sometimes tolerated. A pass was required when away from their master's property.

Convicts were not welcomed by all those living there. Benjamin Franklin was quoted as saying that he would exchange convicts for rattlesnakes.

Not everyone wanted them to return either. One Northumberland woman told her husband when he was sentenced to transportation at the quarter sessions court in Hexham, that though she was sorry, 'she had another ready to replace him'.

In 1775 transportation to Africa was stopped because convicts were dying from starvation and malaria. The American Revolution culminating in the American War of Independence 1775-1782 halted transportation there. Interestingly, Newcastle protested vehemently to George III about the revolt:

2nd December, 1775 – American War of Independence

'The recorder, eight aldermen, the sheriff, fourteen of the common council and other gentlemen and inhabitants amounting to in all 169 persons, signed an address to the King lamenting the deject and revolt of his subjects in America and assuring him of their abhorrence and detestation of so unjustifiable spirit of resistance.'

Criminals were imprisoned, even though sentences of transportation were still passed. The prisons became overcrowded and prisoners were housed in old ships known as 'prison hulks' moored in coastal waters like the Thames. Conditions were appalling.

The 'hulks' were poorly ventilated, overrun with vermin and disease was rife. It was felt an alternative transportation destination needed to be found. In 1788 it was Australia's turn.

Transportation to Australia 1786-1868

Australia became a penal colony from approximately 1786-1868. Apart from thieves, robbers, rapists, murderers and so on, about 1,200 people who were involved in political or social unrest were also transported.

The 752 sentenced for their political actions, as opposed to arsonists, marginal social protesters and poachers' can be divided into:

The 'Swing' Rioters of 1830

The name 'Captain Swing' was written on several threatening letters sent to people like magistrates and parsons and the term 'swing letters' was first used by *The Times* on the 21st October. It is thought 'Captain Swing' was just a fictional character, if he wasn't he was never identified. The letters were used to highlight the increasing difficulties such as the steadily decreasing wages of those who worked on the land as well as genuine concerns about machines causing unemployment. 475 were convicted for machine breaking, arson, receiving or rioting and transported to New South Wales or Van Dieman's Land (Tasmania) from the south east of England.

The Tolpuddle Martyrs

In 1832, Lord Grey the MP for Northumberland, ensured the Great Reform Act was passed. Although it extended the vote in England, it did not grant universal suffrage. Six Tolpuddle men refused to work for less than 10 shillings a week and formed the Friendly Society of Agricultural Labourers in Dorset to protest against steadily decreasing wages.

102 Chartists in 1839, 1842 and 1848

Those who agreed with the People's Charter, published in May 1838 became known as Chartists. They wanted voting by ballot; all males to be able to vote; Parliaments to meet annually; equality of electoral districts: the opportunity for any man to be an MP and members to be paid.

The 18th and 19th centuries saw people turning from the land and agriculture to employment in industrial towns and cities. Communities broke up and crime figures at the time increased. The response by the authorities was to increase the number of crimes on the statute book and impose severe punishments for what we might regard today, as minor crimes.

Criminals were imprisoned, even though sentences of transportation were still passed. The prisons became overcrowded and prisoners were housed in old ships known as 'prison hulks' moored in coastal waters like the Thames. Conditions were appalling. The 'hulks' were poorly ventilated, overrun with vermin and disease was rife. It was felt an alternative transportation destination needed to be found.

Right: A prison hulk with prisoners going on board.

During a period of 80 years, about 158,702 male and female criminals were transported from England and Ireland to Australia. Another 1,321, were from parts of the British Empire. Transportation was at its height in the 1830s. The total of men and women transported during this time was 160,023. Up to 1853 convicts were transported to New South Wales (south east Australia); Norfolk Island (the main island of a group east of the Australia in the Pacific Ocean); Moreton Bay (Queensland, north east Australia); Van Dieman's Land and Western Australia by 1868.

15% of all convicts were women. Out of 84,000 convicts sent to New South Wales 11,500 were women, whilst a further 12,000 were sent to Norfolk Island and Van Dieman's Land. No women were despatched to Western Australia.

Transportation was mainly for 7 years, 14 years or Life.

The names below are taken from the Calendars of Assizes of prisoners held in Durham, Newcastle and Morpeth Gaols and sentenced to transportation from 1786.

A CALENDAR of the PRISONERS that are to be tried at the ASSIZES, 1786. FELONS IN DURHAM GAOL

JOHN DISBURY, committed by the Rev. Robert Thorp, charged with having feloniously stolen in the dwelling house of George Holmes, sundry Articles of Wearing Apparel, the Property of the said George Holmes. – *Seven Years Transportation.*

JOHN SUTCLIFFE, committed by Henry Mills, Esq: charged upon the Oaths of John Marshall and Charles Wright, with having stolen a Silver Pint, the Property of the said John Marshall. – *Seven Years Transportation.*

No trace of Disbury or Sutcliffe can be found after they were convicted at the Durham Assizes. It is important to note that some convicts may have had their sentences commuted, been freed or died in gaol as no record of their transportation or penal servitude in Australia can be found. It was in the convict's interest to hide their background and men often changed their name or the spelling changed either by design or error. Women married and took their husband's surname and so on. There were few churches or churchyards at this time and therefore few church records to check.

Left: HMS 'Sirius', the flagship of the First Fleet to Australia in 1787.

The First Fleet – 13th May, 1787

Commanded by Captain Arthur Phillip, the First Fleet consisted of 11 ships. Six were transport ships the *Alexander, Charlotte, Friendship, Lady Penrhyn, Prince of Wales* and *Scarborough* carrying 717 convicts, 180 of these were women. Two warships and three store-ships also sailed with them to Botany Bay (a bay in Sydney), and 48 convicts died on the way. It took the *Alexander* 251 days and the *Lady Penrhyn* 252 days to arrive in New South Wales. There is no way of checking who stayed in England or died on board because the lists for those supposedly on the fleets were written in England.

Convicts who came from Durham or Newcastle upon Tyne were:

Surname	Christian Name	Trial	Sentence
*Clough	Richard	Durham Assizes 19th July, 1785	7 years. Voyage date February 1787 on the *Alexander* from Portsmouth bound for New South Wales.
*Hall	Elizabeth	Newcastle Assizes 18th January, 1786	7 years. She sailed in February 1787 on the *Lady Penrhyn* from Portsmouth bound for New South Wales.
*M'Laughlin	Charles	Durham Assizes 21st July, 1785	7 years. On February 1787 he was on the *Alexander* from Portsmouth bound for New South Wales.
*Macintire	John	Durham Assizes 20th July, 1785	7 years. He sailed on the *Alexander* from Portsmouth bound for New South Wales
*Shepherd	Robert	Durham Assizes 19th July, 1785	7 years. He set sail on the *Alexander* from Portsmouth bound for New South Wales.
*Sharp/e	George	Durham Assizes 19th July, 1785	7 years. Voyage date February 1787 on the *Alexander* from Portsmouth bound for New South Wales.
*Thompson	William	Durham Assizes 22nd July, 1785	7 years. He set sail on the *Alexander* from Portsmouth bound for New South Wales.
*Welch	John	Durham Assizes 20th July, 1785	7 years. He sailed on the *Alexander* from Portsmouth bound for New South Wales.

*Richard Clough was approximately 26 when he was originally sentenced to death with his partners in crime, *John Stokoe and *George Sharp/e, for stealing 470 shillings. Stokoe, aged about 34 and Sharp/e, about 39, were transported on the same ship at the same time. No occupations were recorded. Stokoe left New South Wales in 1793 and Sharp/e died in 1787.

*Elizabeth Hall was married to mariner William Hall as we see in an account in the *Newcastle Courant*, 21st January, 1786 below:

'At the adjourned Sessions on Wednesday last, the following persons were convicted of petty larceny, and received the following sentences, viz Elizabeth, wife of William Hall, Mariner, ordered to be transported for seven years.'

Elizabeth would appear to have been born in 1768 and was probably 18 when she was sentenced for the crime of 'petit' stealing in Newcastle. She was a servant and described as being 4' 4'' tall, healthy and strong.

Could this be her in the New South Wales Census in 1828? It notes a 78 year old (our Elizabeth would have been 60) Elizabeth Hall residing as a patient in the Liverpool Lunatic Asylum (she had been there since at least 1822) and died in this institution in 1835.

1828 New South Wales, Australian Census

Name	Age	Ship	Sentence	Employment	Residence
Hall Elizabeth	78	Lady Penrhyn	–	Patient in Asylum	Liverpool

*Charles McLaughlin/McEllan/McLennan/MacLaulin was 15 years old when he was sentenced for stealing a purse and 1 shilling. No occupation was recorded. On the 20th April, 1788 he was given 36 lashes for stealing rum. He was also given 36 lashes for 'seditious and threatening words' on the 18th May, 1788. Having stolen eggs, on the 7th August, 1788, he received 36 lashes. On the 5th May, 1790 he suffered a fractured skull and was expected to die. He stole potatoes on the 15th May, 1791 and was sentenced to 6 weeks in irons on 2 weeks ration of corn and water, but on the 12th June punishment stopped. In January 1793 he left New South Wales.

*John Macintire/MacIntire/McIntire was tried for assault and robbery of 5 shillings. He was originally sentenced to death, but was transported for 7 years. He was aged about 32 and no occupation was recorded. He was one of a minority of convicts allowed to carry a gun and was a licensed game killer. The Aboriginal leader Pemulwuy attacked and wounded him on the 10th December, 1788 and he died in the same year.

*Robert Shepherd/Sheppard was approximately 32 when he stole sacks of flour worth 5 shillings. No occupation was recorded. In 1793 he left New South Wales.

George Sharp/e see Richard Cleugh above.

*William/Jeremy Thompson stole a mare worth 160 shillings when he was about 33. He was originally sentenced to death and then transported. He concealed fish and was lashed 25 times. He married Maria Hamilton on the 24th March, 1788. She was tried on the 19th October, 1785 at the Old Bailey for stealing clothing worth 30 shillings. Aged approximately 33, she sailed on the *Lady Penrhyn*. Her occupation was recorded as a lace weaver. On the 29th August 1788, she received 25 strokes of the lash for drunkenness and insolence. William and Mariah had three children. William died in 1805.

*John Welch was aged about 57 when he stole 215 shillings. He was first sentenced to hang, but was transported. No occupation was recorded. It is thought he died in 1794.

Botany Bay was unsuitable as a landing area as there was no fresh water and the harbour was unsafe. The First Fleet arrived at Port Jackson (the harbour where Sydney is located) in January in 1788 and raised the British flag at Sydney Cove (a small bay south of Port Jackson). The surviving convicts, 252 marines and their wives disembarked and from 1788-1823, they made up the population of the Colony of New South Wales. In 1793, the first free settlers arrived.

Women made up 20% of the first transport. Some had been domestic servants in England others were regarded as immoral and prostitutes. Unfortunately some had to become prostitutes to survive as the young pretty girls were usually chosen as servants by the officers and gentry. The majority of female convicts, particularly 'the hardened' and many who were free, were placed in the Female Factory (a textile factory which made a profit) as unassigned women. Some lived in the Factory, others did not. Many, after a few days, became servants for settlers. The children of convicts either stayed with their mothers or went to an orphanage.

Any man wanting to marry a female convict just had to apply so many women were married soon after arrival. The man would take his pick from a line of women in the Factory. He'd drop his handkerchief beside the woman he'd chosen and if she picked it up the marriage was swiftly arranged. Marriage basically freed a woman, as it was thought she would be more useful as a wife and mother.

Male convicts were given work such as carpentry, brick making and farming according to their skills. Educated convicts became bookkeepers for the penal administration.

By the early 1800s, convicts were also being sent directly to Moreton Bay, Norfolk Island, Port Macquarie (New South Wales) and Van Dieman's Land.

Two ships that were part of the First Fleet. On the right is the Sunderland-built 'Borrowdale' and on the left is the 'Lady Penrhyn'.

From 1810 convicts worked for free settlers and small land holders as well as being involved in building work to develop the colonies.

By 1821 land, positions of trust and responsibility were given to a growing number of freed convicts. Only about 6% of the convict population was locked up by the mid 1830s.

The Second Fleet Sailed in 1789

The Second Fleet was an unmitigated disaster. Six ships left England (two were store ships The *Guardian* and *Justinian*). The *Surprize*, *Neptune* and *Scarborough* carried mainly male passengers. The *Lady Juliana* was the first all female transport ship, the first to leave England and the first to arrive in the colony of New South Wales.
It took a year to complete her journey (possibly because the captain did not protect the women from his crew). On arrival the women doubled the female population of Sydney.

Private contractors transported the prisoners and the journey was a nightmare. The *Guardian*, which was full of provisions, struck ice and was unable to complete the voyage. Over 25% (278) of 1250 male prisoners died from the poor rations, unsanitary conditions and general lack of care during the voyage in comparison to 2.8% (48) in the First Fleet

Half of the convicts who arrived needed prompt hospitalisation and approximately 80 died within three weeks of being in Sydney.

Some of the convicts from Durham and Northumberland who sailed on the Second Fleet:

Surname	Christian Name	Trial/Birthplace	Sentence
*Miller	John	Berwick upon Tweed Quarter Sessions. 14th January, 1789	7 years. Voyage in November on the *Surprize*.
*Moreton	William	Northumberland Newcastle upon Tyne Quarter Sessions 24th April, 1789	7 years. Voyage in November, 1789 on the *Neptune*.
*Winship /Winstrip	William	Durham Quarter Sessions 10th January, 1787	14 years. Voyage in November, 1789 on the *Surprize*.

*John Miller appears to have been from Edinburgh and stole two jackets (one was flannel), a silk waistcoat and a pair of breeches from the 'Salmon' fishing smack (a small fishing boat) on the River Tweed at Berwick.

He was also convicted on a separate matter of the theft of a leather pocket book, gold ring and three breast 'broaches'. On the 14th January, 1789, at the Quarter Sessions in Berwick upon Tweed, he was sentenced to seven years transportation and signed a statement saying he was not guilty.

John was taken to Berwick Gaol, then by sea on the 'London Packet' (a ship which primarily carried mail) to London on 3rd April, 1789. On arrival on 10th April he had to board the prison hulk *Stanislaus* (one of numerous old ships used as temporary prisons and moored on the Thames). He was 23 years old. There is no certain record of him in the colony.

*William Moreton was the second mate of a ship on East India Service and described as 5' 9'' tall, thin and dark complexioned.

On 24th April, 1789 he was convicted of obtaining money by false pretences. From the 4th July-12th November he was on the prison hulk *Justitia*. He was 28 years old. He appeared to be one of the lucky survivors of the transport because he landed at Sydney Cove in March 1791. Within 9 months he was involved in a daredevil escape involving 9 male convicts, a woman and two small children. Those who are known are: First Fleet convicts William and Mary Bryant (husband and wife) and Second Fleet convicts: William Allen, Samuel Broom and Nathaniel Lillie.

They stole a boat with a sail, navigation equipment and supplies. It was probably due to Moreton's navigational skills that they reached Timor 69 days later. The Dutch officials treated them as if they were shipwreck survivors. Unfortunately after drunkenly quarrelling with his wife, Bryant betrayed them. They were arrested and handed to the British authorities and sent back to Britain for retrials. Sadly Moreton died in 1791 or early 1792 at sea between Batavia and Cape Town.

A convict settlement on Norfolk Island, Australia.

*William Winship/Winstrip was 25 years old when he was sentenced at the Durham Quarter Sessions to 14 years transportation on 10th January, 1787. His crime was receiving stolen metal and nails from Cuthbert Winship and Robert Oliver. Robert Oliver was sentenced to seven years transportation and arrived in the colony in 1791. Cuthbert Winship does not appear to have been arrested. (See his previous offences below).

Records show that Durham Gaol was infested with bugs at this time so William and Robert were likely to be thankful to be taken to 'Sutherland' (probably Sunderland) with eight other convicts on 23rd April, 1787 from where they sailed to London.

William boarded the *Ceres* a prison hulk in the Thames, on 28th April. He remained in it when it sailed to Langstone Harbour, Portsmouth some months afterwards. He impressed a construction works supervisor so much when he worked in a gang of pilers, his name was placed on a list of those the superintendent wanted to keep in England. However, in the end he was transported in 1789 and landed at Sydney Cove. He died five months later on the 10th December, 1790 at Parramata.

NB: Cuthbert Winship had a gaol record. In April 1784 he stole geese and was sentenced to gaol and to be, 'whipe around the market place on 1st May next'; on August 1784 he was found not guilty of burglary.

Despite the horrific conditions the prisoners experienced during their transportation, many survived and their endeavours supported the new settlement.
   The British government could not hide the dreadful facts of the voyage and some of those held responsible were dealt with under the law. There was certainly more care taken over the choice of contractors and officers for future transports, however, conditions though slightly improved, remained atrocious.

Australian Sources

Department of Education – Archives of Tasmania

NSW Registry of Births, Deaths and Marriages – Indexes

www.bdm.nsw.gov.au

Western Australia Registry of Births, Deaths and Marriages – Indexes

www.bdm.dotag.wa.gov.au

Australian Joint Copying Project:

Great Britain. Home Office; State Library of Queensland; Publisher: Canberra A.C.T. Australian Joint Copying Project. Part of Criminal: Convict transportation registers (HO 11).

Microfilm Roll 93, Class and Piece Number HO11/19, Page Number 239 (122)

Microfilm Roll 93, Class and Piece Number HO11/18, page Number 366.

Australian Convict Transportation Registers First Fleet 1787-1788

Australian Convict Transportation Registers Second Fleet 1789-1790

Australian Convict Third Fleet Transportation Registers 1791

Australian Convict Transportation Registers Other Fleets & Ships 1791-1868

New South Wales Australian Census 1828 (TNA Copy)

Conclusion

Lack of education and the harsh living and social conditions of the past are often used as a justification for the crimes that took place at that time, however, crime still exists today even though there have been vast improvements in all these areas.
   Perhaps we just need a more caring society; one that allows a parent, whether rich or poor to stay at home and bring up children if that is their wish; one where respect for self, family, others and their property is positively promoted by everyone.
   There is indecision today about punishment for criminals. Some people cling to the notion that longer prison sentences will do the trick. This was patently not the case for many in the past. Others call for alternatives to imprisonment and a hopeful reduction in reoffending figures.
   Whatever decision is reached it must be seen to ensure justice for both victim and offender.

Bibliography

Anderson, M. (2005). *Executions & Hangings in MORPETH & NEWCASTLE*, Wharncliffe Books.

Charlton, R.J. (1880). *Newcastle Town* (Reissued in 1950 as *Charlton's History of Newcastle upon Tyne Its Growth and Achievement*, Harold Hull, Newcastle upon Tyne).

Flynn, M. (1993). *The Second Fleet: Britain's Grim Convict Armada of 1790*, Library of Australian History, Sydney.

Green, N. (No Date). *TOUGH TIMES & GRISLY CRIMES, A HISTORY OF CRIME in Northumberland and Durham*, Nigel Green Media.

Harrison, F. (1912). *A History of Newcastle upon Tyne*, Hewitt and Rudge.

Histon, V. (2001). *GHOSTS of Grainger Town Further tales from Newcastle's Darker Side*, City of Newcastle upon Tyne Libraries and Information Service, Tyne Bridge Publishing.

Histon, V. (2006). *Unlocking the QUAYSIDE Newcastle Gateshead's historic waterfront explored*, City of Newcastle upon Tyne Libraries and Information Service, Tyne Bridge Publishing.

Liddell, T. (2004). *OTHERWORLD NORTH EAST Ghosts and Hauntings Explored*, City of Newcastle upon Tyne Libraries and Information Service, Tyne Bridge Publishing.

MacDonald Fraser, G. (1986). *The Steel Bonnets The Story of the Anglo-Scottish Border Reivers*, HarperCollins.

Mackenzie, E.A. (1827). *A descriptive and historical account of the town and country of Newcastle upon Tyne, including the borough of Gateshead*. (3 vols), Mackenzie & Dent.

Morgan, A. (2007). *Victorian Panorama*, City of Newcastle upon Tyne Libraries and Information Service, Tyne Bridge Publishing.

Morgan, G. & Rushton, P. (1998). *Rogues, thieves and the rule of law – The problem of law enforcement in north-east England, 1718-1800*, UCL Press.

Newman, S. (2005). *Newcastle upon Tyne*, Sanderson Books Limited.

Redfern, B. (2006). *Victorian Villains Prisoners from Newcastle Gaol 1871-1873*, City of Newcastle upon Tyne Newcastle Libraries and Information Service, Tyne Bridge Publishing.

Ritson, D. W. (2009). *HAUNTED NEWCASTLE*, The History Press.

Robinson, P. (1988). *The Women of Botany Bay 1788-1828, Volume 1*, Oxford University Press.

Winter, P., Milne, D., Brown, J., Rushworth, A. (1989). *Newcastle upon Tyne*, Northern Heritage Consultancy Ltd.

Newspapers and Periodicals

The Gentleman's Magazine and Historical Chronicle
The Leeds Mercury
The Newcastle Chronicle
The Newcastle Courant

Tyne and Wear Archive Service

Newcastle Gaol, Collection of Prison Forms and Photographs 1873

Websites

www.localhistories.org
www.ancestry.co.uk
www.policememorial.org.uk
www.british-history.ac.uk
www.sl.nsw.gov.au
www.chs.revues.org

Also available from Summerhill Books

'Offbeat'

Memories of Tynemouth Borough Police and the Communities it served –
North Shields, Tynemouth & Cullercoats